Clearing the Air

Juanita LA

Published by Alex Corma, 2024.

While every precaution has been taken in the preparation of this book, the publisher assumes no responsibility for errors or omissions, or for damages resulting from the use of the information contained herein.

CLEARING THE AIR

First edition. October 21, 2024.

Copyright © 2024 Juanita LA.

ISBN: 979-8227849410

Written by Juanita LA.

Introduction

The harmful effects of smoking on our health and wellness are well-documented. From lung cancer to heart disease, smoking has been linked to a wide range of serious health issues that can significantly impact our quality of life. As a result, there has been a growing movement towards embracing a smoke-free future in order to promote optimal health and wellness for individuals and communities around the world.

Over the years, I have dedicated my career to researching and writing about the importance of clearing the air of tobacco smoke and the benefits of embracing a smoke-free lifestyle. Through my work, I have seen firsthand the devastating impact that smoking can have on individuals and their loved ones. From witnessing the struggles of those trying to quit, to understanding the toll that smoking-related illnesses can take on families, it has become increasingly clear to me that we must do everything in our power to create a healthier, smoke-free future for all.

In my bestselling books, I have delved into the scientific research surrounding the dangers of smoking, as well as the societal and economic implications of tobacco use. I have also explored the latest advancements in smoking cessation methods and the positive outcomes that can be achieved by individuals who make the decision to quit. Through my research, I have become a staunch advocate for the promotion of smoke-free environments and the implementation of policies that support individuals in their efforts to lead healthier, smoke-free lives.

The benefits of embracing a smoke-free future extend far beyond just the individual level. By reducing smoking rates and creating smoke-free environments, we can significantly improve public health outcomes and reduce the burden on healthcare systems. Additionally, promoting smoke-free policies can lead to cleaner air and a healthier environment for all, which has a positive impact on the wellbeing of communities as a whole.

One of the key aspects of embracing a smoke-free future is the importance of education and awareness. By providing individuals with the knowledge and resources they need to understand the dangers of smoking and the benefits of quitting, we can empower them to make informed decisions about their health. This includes educating individuals on the various smoking cessation methods available to them, as well as the support systems that can help them through the quitting process. By arming individuals with the tools they need to make positive changes in their lives, we can pave the way for a healthier, smoke-free future for all.

In the pages that follow, I will explore the various facets of embracing a smoke-free future, from the individual benefits of quitting smoking to the broader societal and environmental implications of reducing tobacco use. I will also share real-life stories of individuals who have successfully quit smoking and the positive impact it has had on their lives. Through this exploration, I hope to inspire and empower readers to make positive changes in their own lives and to advocate for smoke-free policies in their communities.

As we continue to move towards a smoke-free future, it is my hope that this book will serve as a valuable resource for individuals and communities looking to improve their health and wellness by clearing the air of tobacco smoke. Together, we can create a healthier, smoke-free future for all.

Chapter 1: The Dangers of Smoking

The health risks associated with smoking

As we delve into the topic of smoking and its impact on health, it is crucial to first understand the myriad of health risks associated with this habit. Smoking is a leading cause of various serious health conditions, including lung cancer, heart disease, and respiratory issues. The harmful chemicals present in tobacco smoke, such as nicotine and tar, can significantly damage the lungs and cardiovascular system over time. In addition, smoking can also increase the risk of developing other types of cancer, such as throat, bladder, and pancreatic cancer.

Furthermore, smoking has been linked to a range of other health problems, including chronic obstructive pulmonary disease (COPD), emphysema, and bronchitis. These conditions can lead to significant breathing difficulties, reduced lung function, and decreased quality of life. Moreover, smoking can weaken the immune system, making individuals more susceptible to infections and illnesses. It can also have detrimental effects on reproductive health, leading to fertility issues and complications during pregnancy.

The impact of smoking extends beyond the individual's health, affecting those around them as well. Secondhand smoke exposure can pose serious health risks to non-smokers, particularly children and pregnant women. It can increase the risk of respiratory infections, asthma, sudden infant death syndrome (SIDS), and other adverse health outcomes.

It is important to recognize that the health risks associated with smoking are not limited to physical health. Smoking can also have a significant impact on mental health, contributing to increased stress, anxiety, and depression. The addictive nature of nicotine can further exacerbate these mental health challenges, creating a vicious cycle that is difficult to break.

In conclusion, the health risks associated with smoking are extensive and far-reaching. From damaging the lungs and cardiovascular system to increasing the risk of various cancers, smoking poses a significant threat to overall health and well-being. It is essential for individuals to understand these risks and make informed decisions about their smoking habits. Embracing a smoke-free future is not only beneficial for personal health but also for the health of those around us. It is a step towards optimal health and wellness for individuals, families, and communities.

Secondhand smoke and its effects on non

Secondhand smoke is a serious health concern that affects non-smokers in various ways. When non-smokers are exposed to secondhand smoke, they inhale the same harmful chemicals and toxins that smokers do. This exposure increases their risk of developing a wide range of health problems, including respiratory infections, asthma, lung cancer, and heart disease.

The effects of secondhand smoke on non-smokers can be particularly harmful for children, pregnant women, and individuals with pre-existing health conditions. Children who are exposed to secondhand smoke are at a higher risk of developing asthma, respiratory infections, and sudden infant death syndrome (SIDS). Pregnant women who are exposed to secondhand smoke are more likely to experience complications during pregnancy and have babies with low birth weight.

In addition to these immediate health effects, secondhand smoke exposure can also have long-term consequences for non-smokers. Studies have shown that non-smokers who are regularly exposed to secondhand smoke have an increased risk of developing lung cancer and heart disease. This is because the chemicals and toxins in secondhand smoke can damage the cells in the body and contribute to the development of these serious health conditions.

It is important for non-smokers to take proactive steps to protect themselves and their loved ones from secondhand smoke exposure. This can include implementing smoke-free policies in the home and workplace, advocating for smoke-free public spaces, and avoiding places where smoking is permitted. By taking these measures, non-smokers can reduce their risk of experiencing the harmful effects of secondhand smoke and promote a healthier, smoke-free future for themselves and future generations.

In conclusion, secondhand smoke poses a significant threat to the health and well-being of non-smokers. The harmful chemicals and toxins in secondhand smoke can lead to a wide range of health problems, including respiratory infections, asthma, lung cancer, and heart disease. It is crucial for non-smokers to be aware of the risks associated with secondhand smoke exposure and take proactive steps to protect themselves and their loved ones. By embracing a smoke-free future, non-smokers can promote optimal health and wellness for themselves and future generations.

The financial burden of smoking on individuals and society

As a seasoned copywriter with extensive knowledge on the subject of "Clearing the Air: Embracing a Smoke-Free Future for Optimal Health and Wellness", I understand the profound impact that smoking has on both individuals and society as a whole. In this chapter, I will delve into the financial burden of smoking, shedding light on the detrimental effects it has on personal finances and the economy.

First and foremost, the cost of smoking takes a significant toll on individuals' wallets. From purchasing cigarettes to covering medical expenses related to smoking-related illnesses, the financial implications can be staggering. The ongoing expense of sustaining a smoking habit can drain one's resources, leading to financial strain and hardship. Moreover, the long-term health consequences of smoking can result in substantial medical bills, further exacerbating the financial burden on individuals and their families.

Beyond the individual level, smoking also places a substantial economic burden on society as a whole. The costs associated with treating smoking-related illnesses place a heavy demand on healthcare systems, resulting in increased healthcare expenditures. Additionally, lost productivity due to smoking-related illnesses and premature deaths further adds to the economic impact. This not only affects the workforce but also places strain on government resources and taxpayer funds.

Furthermore, the environmental impact of smoking, such as the cost of cleaning up cigarette litter and addressing fire hazards caused by smoking, also contributes to the overall financial burden on society. These costs are often overlooked but can add up significantly over time, placing an additional strain on public resources.

In conclusion, the financial burden of smoking is substantial, impacting both individuals and society at large. From the personal cost of sustaining a smoking habit to the broader economic implications of healthcare expenditures and lost productivity, the financial toll of smoking is undeniable. It is imperative that we address this issue and work towards a smoke-free future for the betterment of our health and wellness, as well as the economic well-being of our society.

The impact of smoking on the environment

Smoking has long been recognized as a significant public health concern, with its detrimental effects on individual health well-documented. However, the impact of smoking on the environment is often overlooked, despite its far-reaching implications. The environmental consequences of smoking are multifaceted and profound, affecting air and water quality, as well as contributing to deforestation and littering.

One of the most evident environmental impacts of smoking is air pollution. Cigarette smoke contains thousands of chemicals, many of which are released into the air when a cigarette is lit. These chemicals, including carbon monoxide, formaldehyde, and ammonia, can linger in the air for extended periods, contributing to air pollution. This pollution can have serious consequences for both the environment and human health, as it can exacerbate respiratory conditions and contribute to the formation of smog.

In addition to air pollution, smoking also has a significant impact on water quality. Cigarette butts, which are the most commonly littered item in the world, are not only unsightly but also pose a serious threat to aquatic ecosystems. These filters are made of a type of plastic called cellulose acetate, which can take years to break down. When discarded improperly, cigarette butts often end up in waterways, where they can leach toxic chemicals and pose a hazard to marine life.

Furthermore, the production of tobacco and the manufacturing of cigarettes also have environmental consequences. Tobacco cultivation often involves the use of large amounts of pesticides and fertilizers, which can contaminate soil and water sources. Additionally, the curing and drying of tobacco leaves require significant amounts of fuel, contributing to carbon emissions and deforestation. The production of cigarettes also generates a substantial amount of waste and packaging, further contributing to environmental degradation.

When considering the impact of smoking on the environment, it is crucial to recognize the collective responsibility to address this issue. Individuals, governments, and businesses all have a role to play in mitigating the environmental consequences of smoking. Public education and awareness campaigns can help to reduce the prevalence of smoking and discourage littering. Additionally, policies and regulations aimed at reducing tobacco consumption and promoting environmentally friendly alternatives can contribute to a smoke-free future for optimal health and wellness.

In conclusion, the impact of smoking on the environment is far-reaching and multifaceted. From air and water pollution to deforestation and littering, the environmental consequences of smoking are significant and cannot be ignored. Addressing these issues requires collective efforts and a commitment to promoting a smoke-free future for the betterment of both human health and the environment. By recognizing the environmental impact of smoking and taking action to address it, we can strive towards a healthier, more sustainable future for all.

Chapter 2: The Benefits of Quitting Smoking

Improved lung function and respiratory health

As we continue to explore the benefits of embracing a smoke-free future, it's essential to delve into the significant improvements in lung function and respiratory health that come with this decision. The impact of smoking on the respiratory system is well-documented, with the harmful chemicals and toxins in cigarette smoke causing extensive damage to the lungs over time. However, by choosing to live smoke-free, individuals can experience a remarkable transformation in their lung function and overall respiratory well-being.

One of the most notable improvements that individuals can expect to see is increased lung capacity. Smoking restricts the airways and damages the delicate lung tissue, leading to reduced lung function and a decreased ability to breathe deeply. By eliminating exposure to harmful smoke, the lungs can begin to repair themselves, resulting in improved airflow and increased lung capacity. This means that individuals will be able to take deeper breaths, allowing for more efficient oxygen exchange and better overall respiratory function.

In addition to increased lung capacity, quitting smoking can also lead to a decrease in respiratory symptoms. Many smokers experience chronic coughing, wheezing, and shortness of breath as a result of their habit. However, by choosing to embrace a smoke-free lifestyle, individuals may notice a significant reduction in these symptoms. The body's natural healing processes can work to repair the damage caused by smoking, leading to clearer airways and improved respiratory function.

Furthermore, individuals who choose to live smoke-free may also experience a reduced risk of developing respiratory illnesses and conditions. Smoking is a known risk factor for a wide range of respiratory issues, including chronic obstructive pulmonary disease

(COPD), emphysema, and chronic bronchitis. By eliminating exposure to smoke, individuals can significantly lower their risk of developing these debilitating conditions, allowing them to enjoy better respiratory health and a higher quality of life.

Another crucial aspect of improved lung function and respiratory health is the potential for enhanced physical performance. Smoking can have a detrimental impact on athletic performance and overall physical endurance, as it impairs the body's ability to efficiently transport oxygen to the muscles. By quitting smoking and embracing a smoke-free lifestyle, individuals can experience improved physical performance, increased stamina, and a greater overall sense of well-being.

In conclusion, the decision to live smoke-free can have a profound and positive impact on lung function and respiratory health. By eliminating exposure to harmful smoke, individuals can experience increased lung capacity, a reduction in respiratory symptoms, a decreased risk of developing respiratory illnesses, and improved physical performance. These benefits are just a few of the many reasons to embrace a smoke-free future for optimal health and wellness. With dedication and commitment to a smoke-free lifestyle, individuals can look forward to enjoying improved lung function and respiratory well-being for years to come.

Reduced risk of heart disease and cancer

As we continue to delve into the numerous benefits of embracing a smoke-free future, it is crucial to shed light on the significantly reduced risk of heart disease and cancer. The detrimental effects of smoking on cardiovascular health are well-documented, with numerous studies linking tobacco use to an increased risk of heart disease. When individuals inhale the toxic chemicals present in cigarette smoke, their blood vessels constrict, leading to increased blood pressure and reduced blood flow to the heart. Over time, this can result in the buildup of fatty deposits in the arteries, a condition known as atherosclerosis, which significantly raises the risk of heart attacks and strokes.

Moreover, the correlation between smoking and cancer cannot be overstated. Tobacco smoke contains a multitude of carcinogens that can damage the DNA in cells, leading to the uncontrollable growth of cancerous tumors. Lung cancer is the most well-known consequence of smoking, with the majority of cases directly attributed to tobacco use. However, the harmful effects of smoking extend far beyond the lungs, as it has been linked to an increased risk of developing various other types of cancer, including throat, mouth, esophagus, bladder, kidney, pancreas, and cervix cancer, among others.

Fortunately, quitting smoking or avoiding tobacco use altogether can significantly reduce the risk of developing heart disease and cancer. Research has shown that individuals who quit smoking can experience a rapid improvement in cardiovascular health, with a reduced risk of heart attacks and strokes within just a few years of quitting. Furthermore, the risk of developing cancer also decreases over time, providing further incentive for individuals to embrace a smoke-free lifestyle.

In addition to the individual health benefits, embracing a smoke-free future also has broader societal implications. By reducing the prevalence of smoking, we can alleviate the burden on healthcare systems, freeing up resources to tackle other pressing health issues. Furthermore, the reduction in smoking-related illnesses can lead to a healthier, more productive workforce, benefiting the economy as a whole.

In conclusion, the reduced risk of heart disease and cancer is a compelling reason to embrace a smoke-free future. By making the choice to quit smoking or avoid tobacco use altogether, individuals can significantly improve their overall health and well-being, while also contributing to a healthier society at large. It is imperative that we continue to raise awareness about the detrimental effects of smoking and provide support for those looking to make positive changes in their lives. Embracing a smoke-free future is not just a personal decision, but a collective commitment to optimal health and wellness for all.

Increased life expectancy and overall wellness

As we continue to progress towards a smoke-free future, one of the most significant benefits we can anticipate is the increased life expectancy and overall wellness of the population. The detrimental effects of smoking on health are well-documented, and by embracing a smoke-free lifestyle, individuals can significantly improve their chances of living a longer and healthier life.

Research has consistently shown that smoking is a leading cause of preventable death worldwide. By quitting smoking and creating smoke-free environments, individuals can reduce their risk of developing serious health conditions such as heart disease, stroke, and various forms of cancer. This, in turn, can lead to a substantial increase in life expectancy and overall wellness.

By eliminating exposure to secondhand smoke, not only do non-smokers benefit from a reduced risk of developing smoking-related illnesses, but the overall health of the community also improves. This is particularly important for vulnerable populations such as children, the elderly, and individuals with pre-existing health conditions. Creating smoke-free environments can lead to a significant decrease in healthcare costs and an increase in productivity, as individuals are able to lead healthier and more active lives.

In addition to the physical health benefits, embracing a smoke-free future can also have a positive impact on mental health and well-being. Smoking has been linked to an increased risk of depression, anxiety, and other mental health disorders. By choosing to live a smoke-free lifestyle, individuals can experience improved mental clarity, reduced stress, and an overall sense of well-being.

Furthermore, as smoking is a major contributor to air pollution, embracing a smoke-free future can lead to cleaner air and a healthier environment for all. This can have far-reaching effects on public health, as cleaner air can reduce the incidence of respiratory illnesses and other health conditions related to air pollution.

In conclusion, the benefits of embracing a smoke-free future are clear. By reducing exposure to secondhand smoke, individuals can improve their overall health and increase their life expectancy. This, in turn, can lead to a healthier and more productive society, with reduced healthcare costs and improved mental well-being. It is imperative that we continue to promote smoke-free environments and support individuals in their journey towards a healthier, smoke-free lifestyle.

Financial savings from not purchasing cigarettes

As we delve into the advantages of embracing a smoke-free future, one of the most compelling benefits is the substantial financial savings that come from not purchasing cigarettes. For many individuals, the cost of smoking can take a significant toll on their wallets. By choosing to forgo the expense of cigarettes, individuals can redirect those funds to other areas of their lives, such as savings, investments, or experiences that contribute to their overall well-being.

The financial impact of smoking can be staggering. The cost of a pack of cigarettes can add up quickly, especially for those who smoke multiple packs a day. When considering the long-term effects of this habit, the total expenditure on cigarettes can amount to a substantial sum over the course of a year. By breaking free from this costly habit, individuals can effectively reclaim their financial resources and allocate them towards more meaningful and fulfilling pursuits.

In addition to the direct cost of purchasing cigarettes, there are also indirect financial burdens associated with smoking. These can include increased healthcare expenses due to smoking-related illnesses, higher insurance premiums, and lost productivity from smoking breaks or absenteeism. By eliminating these financial burdens, individuals can enjoy a greater sense of financial security and stability.

Furthermore, the decision to quit smoking can have a positive impact on one's overall financial well-being. As individuals embrace a smoke-free lifestyle, they are likely to experience improved health and wellness, which can lead to reduced healthcare costs and a lower risk of chronic diseases. This, in turn, can translate into long-term savings and a better quality of life.

When considering the financial savings from not purchasing cigarettes, it is important to acknowledge the broader economic benefits as well. A reduction in smoking rates can lead to lower healthcare costs for society as a whole, as well as decreased productivity losses and a healthier workforce. This can have a positive ripple effect on the economy, contributing to a more prosperous and sustainable future for all.

In conclusion, the financial savings from not purchasing cigarettes are undeniable. By choosing to embrace a smoke-free future, individuals can free themselves from the financial burden of smoking and redirect those resources towards a more fulfilling and prosperous life. The benefits extend beyond personal finances, encompassing broader economic advantages that can contribute to a healthier and more vibrant society. Embracing a smoke-free future is not just about improving health and wellness, but also about securing a more stable and prosperous financial future for oneself and for society as a whole.

Chapter 3: Creating a Smoke-Free Environment

Implementing smoke

As we continue to embrace a smoke-free future, the implementation of smoke-free policies becomes crucial for achieving optimal health and wellness. The adoption of such policies in various settings, including public spaces, workplaces, and residential areas, is imperative in creating an environment that promotes clean air and reduces the harmful effects of secondhand smoke on individuals.

One of the key strategies for implementing smoke-free policies is to educate the public about the benefits of a smoke-free environment. This involves raising awareness about the health risks associated with exposure to secondhand smoke and highlighting the positive impact of smoke-free policies on overall well-being. By providing accurate information and engaging in public outreach efforts, it is possible to garner support for the adoption of smoke-free policies at the local, regional, and national levels.

Furthermore, collaboration with stakeholders such as government agencies, businesses, healthcare organizations, and community groups is essential for the successful implementation of smoke-free policies. By working together, these stakeholders can develop and enforce regulations that prohibit smoking in designated areas, establish smoke-free zones, and provide resources to support individuals in their efforts to quit smoking. This collaborative approach fosters a sense of shared responsibility and commitment to creating a healthier and smoke-free environment for all.

In addition to education and collaboration, the enforcement of smoke-free policies is essential for ensuring compliance and promoting a culture of respect for smoke-free regulations. This involves the establishment of clear guidelines, monitoring and enforcement mechanisms, and the imposition of penalties for non-compliance. By holding individuals and organizations accountable for their actions, it is possible to create a strong deterrent against smoking in prohibited areas and promote a culture of compliance with smoke-free policies.

Another important aspect of implementing smoke-free policies is the provision of support for individuals who smoke and wish to quit. This includes access to smoking cessation programs, counseling services, and resources to help individuals overcome nicotine addiction and transition to a smoke-free lifestyle. By offering support and assistance, it is possible to empower individuals to take control of their health and make positive changes that contribute to a smoke-free future.

In conclusion, the implementation of smoke-free policies is a critical step towards creating a healthier and cleaner environment for all. By focusing on education, collaboration, enforcement, and support, it is possible to achieve widespread adoption of smoke-free policies and promote optimal health and wellness for individuals and communities. As we continue to work towards a smoke-free future, let us remain committed to our efforts and strive to create a world where clean air and well-being are prioritized for the benefit of all.

Providing resources and support for individuals looking to quit smoking

Quitting smoking is a challenging journey that requires resources and support to be successful. There are many individuals who want to quit smoking but struggle to find the right tools and assistance to help them along the way. It's important to provide a variety of resources and support systems to cater to the diverse needs of those looking to embrace a smoke-free future. One of the most effective resources for individuals looking to quit smoking is counseling. Counseling provides a supportive environment for individuals to explore their reasons for smoking and develop strategies to overcome their addiction. Counselors can also provide guidance on coping mechanisms and stress management techniques to help individuals navigate the challenges of quitting.

In addition to counseling, support groups are another valuable resource for individuals looking to quit smoking. Support groups offer a sense of community and shared experiences, which can be incredibly empowering for those on their journey to a smoke-free lifestyle. Being able to connect with others who are also striving to quit smoking can provide a sense of solidarity and motivation. Support groups also provide a platform for individuals to share their triumphs and setbacks, and to receive encouragement and advice from others who understand their struggles.

Another important resource for individuals looking to quit smoking is access to nicotine replacement therapies (NRTs) and other medication options. NRTs, such as nicotine patches, gum, and lozenges, can help individuals manage their nicotine cravings and withdrawal symptoms as they work towards quitting smoking. Additionally, prescription medications, such as bupropion and varenicline, can also be effective in supporting individuals through their quit journey. It's essential for individuals to have access to these options and to receive guidance from healthcare professionals on the most suitable methods for their needs.

Moreover, digital resources and mobile applications can also be valuable tools for individuals looking to quit smoking. There are numerous apps and online platforms that provide personalized support, tracking tools, and motivational content to help individuals stay on track with their quit goals. These resources can be especially beneficial for individuals who may not have easy access to in-person support or who prefer a more discreet approach to quitting smoking.

Furthermore, employers and workplaces can play a significant role in supporting individuals looking to quit smoking. Offering smoking cessation programs, incentives for quitting, and creating smoke-free environments can all contribute to a supportive workplace culture that encourages and facilitates smoking cessation. Employers can also provide resources such as access to counseling, NRTs, and educational materials to support their employees in their quit journey.

In conclusion, providing resources and support for individuals looking to quit smoking is crucial for promoting optimal health and wellness. Counseling, support groups, NRTs, medication options, digital resources, and workplace initiatives all play a vital role in empowering individuals to embrace a smoke-free future. By offering a range of resources and support systems, we can create a more inclusive and effective approach to smoking cessation, ultimately leading to improved health outcomes for individuals and communities.

Educating the public on the benefits of a smoke

As a seasoned copywriter specializing in the promotion of smoke-free living, I understand the importance of educating the public on the numerous benefits of embracing a smoke-free future. It is crucial to communicate the advantages of this lifestyle choice in a clear and compelling manner in order to inspire positive change and improve public health and wellness.

First and foremost, it is essential to emphasize the significant impact that smoking has on overall health. By choosing to live smoke-free, individuals can reduce their risk of developing serious health conditions such as lung cancer, heart disease, and respiratory illnesses. Furthermore, embracing a smoke-free lifestyle can lead to improved lung function, increased energy levels, and a reduced risk of premature aging and skin damage.

In addition to the physical health benefits, it is important to highlight the positive effects of a smoke-free environment on mental and emotional well-being. Studies have shown that individuals who live in smoke-free environments experience lower levels of stress, anxiety, and depression. By promoting smoke-free living, we can help create healthier, happier communities where individuals can thrive and reach their full potential.

Another key aspect of educating the public on the benefits of a smoke-free future is raising awareness of the environmental impact of smoking. Cigarette smoke contains harmful chemicals that can pollute the air and water, harm wildlife, and contribute to environmental degradation. By choosing to live smoke-free, individuals can help protect the environment and preserve natural resources for future generations.

Furthermore, promoting smoke-free living can have a positive impact on the economy. The costs associated with smoking-related healthcare, lost productivity, and environmental cleanup are significant. By reducing the prevalence of smoking, we can alleviate the burden on healthcare systems, increase productivity in the workforce, and save valuable resources that can be allocated to other important areas of society.

In conclusion, educating the public on the benefits of a smoke-free future is essential for promoting optimal health and wellness. By communicating the positive impact on physical health, mental and emotional well-being, the environment, and the economy, we can inspire individuals to make informed choices that lead to a healthier, more sustainable future. It is through clear and compelling education that we can empower individuals to embrace a smoke-free lifestyle and reap the numerous rewards it offers.

Encouraging businesses to adopt smoke

As we embrace a smoke-free future for optimal health and wellness, it is crucial for businesses to adopt smoke-free policies within their establishments. Encouraging businesses to implement smoke-free environments not only promotes a healthier workplace for employees and customers but also aligns with the global movement towards a cleaner and healthier lifestyle.

First and foremost, businesses have a responsibility to provide a safe and healthy environment for their employees. By adopting smoke-free policies, businesses can protect their employees from the harmful effects of secondhand smoke, which has been proven to cause serious health issues such as lung cancer, heart disease, and respiratory infections. Creating a smoke-free workplace not only improves the overall health and well-being of employees but also demonstrates a commitment to their safety and welfare.

Furthermore, implementing smoke-free policies can have a positive impact on the overall image and reputation of a business. In today's society, consumers are increasingly conscious of the health and wellness practices of the businesses they support. By promoting a smoke-free environment, businesses can attract health-conscious customers who appreciate and prioritize a clean and healthy atmosphere. This can lead to increased customer loyalty and positive word-of-mouth marketing, ultimately benefiting the business's bottom line.

In addition, embracing a smoke-free future can contribute to a more productive and efficient workplace. Studies have shown that exposure to secondhand smoke can impair cognitive function and decrease productivity. By eliminating smoking in the workplace, businesses can create a more conducive environment for focus and productivity, ultimately leading to improved performance and results.

It is also important to recognize the legal and regulatory benefits of adopting smoke-free policies. Many jurisdictions have implemented laws and regulations that restrict smoking in public spaces, including businesses. By proactively implementing smoke-free policies, businesses can ensure compliance with these regulations and avoid potential legal issues and fines. This demonstrates a commitment to upholding the law and being a responsible corporate citizen.

Moreover, embracing a smoke-free environment can have positive effects on the physical infrastructure of a business. Smoke-free policies can help prevent the buildup of smoke residue and odors, which can be difficult and costly to remove from indoor spaces. By maintaining a smoke-free environment, businesses can preserve the cleanliness and integrity of their facilities, ultimately reducing maintenance and cleaning costs.

In conclusion, encouraging businesses to adopt smoke-free policies is not only a matter of promoting health and wellness but also a strategic decision that can benefit the overall well-being and success of the business. By prioritizing the health and safety of employees and customers, businesses can create a more attractive and productive environment while also ensuring compliance with regulations and reducing operational costs. Embracing a smoke-free future is not only a responsible choice but also a smart business decision.

Chapter 4: The Role of Government and Policy

The importance of government regulations on tobacco products

As we continue to strive towards a smoke-free future for optimal health and wellness, it is essential to recognize the critical role that government regulations play in the control and reduction of tobacco products. These regulations are put in place to protect public health, reduce the prevalence of smoking, and ultimately create a safer, healthier environment for all individuals.

Government regulations on tobacco products encompass a wide range of measures, including restrictions on advertising and promotion, taxation, packaging and labeling requirements, and bans on smoking in public places. These regulations are designed to limit the accessibility and appeal of tobacco products, particularly to young people, and to educate and inform the public about the health risks associated with smoking.

One of the most significant impacts of government regulations on tobacco products is the reduction in smoking rates. Studies have shown that higher taxes on tobacco products, for example, have been effective in decreasing tobacco consumption. By increasing the cost of cigarettes, governments can discourage individuals from purchasing and using tobacco products, particularly among younger and lower-income populations.

In addition to taxation, restrictions on advertising and promotion are also crucial in reducing the appeal and uptake of smoking, particularly among young people. Government regulations often prohibit tobacco companies from advertising their products in certain media outlets, sponsoring events, or using misleading or deceptive marketing tactics. By limiting the exposure to tobacco advertisements, especially among vulnerable populations, governments can prevent the initiation of smoking and reduce overall smoking rates.

Furthermore, packaging and labeling requirements play a vital role in informing consumers about the health risks associated with tobacco use. Graphic health warnings on cigarette packs, for example, have been proven to be effective in increasing awareness of the harmful effects of smoking and encouraging smokers to quit. By mandating the inclusion of prominent health warnings and information on tobacco packaging, governments can empower individuals to make informed decisions about their health and well-being.

Bans on smoking in public places are another essential aspect of government regulations on tobacco products. These bans not only protect non-smokers from exposure to secondhand smoke but also create a supportive environment for smokers who want to quit. By implementing smoke-free policies in public spaces, governments can encourage and support individuals in their efforts to reduce or quit smoking, ultimately contributing to improved public health and well-being.

It is important to note that while government regulations play a crucial role in reducing tobacco use and promoting a smoke-free future, they must be accompanied by other comprehensive tobacco control measures. These may include public education and awareness campaigns, smoking cessation programs, and support for alternative nicotine delivery systems, such as electronic cigarettes. By combining various strategies and interventions, governments can maximize their efforts to reduce the prevalence of smoking and create a healthier, smoke-free society.

In conclusion, government regulations on tobacco products are essential for advancing our goal of embracing a smoke-free future for optimal health and wellness. These regulations are designed to protect public health, reduce smoking rates, and create a safer, healthier environment for all individuals. By implementing measures such as taxation, advertising restrictions, packaging and labeling requirements, and bans on smoking in public places, governments can effectively control and reduce the use of tobacco products, ultimately improving the health and well-being of their populations. It is imperative that governments continue to prioritize and strengthen their efforts in tobacco control, working towards a future where tobacco-related diseases are a thing of the past.

Funding for smoking cessation programs and public health campaigns

As we look towards a smoke-free future, it is crucial to address the issue of funding for smoking cessation programs and public health campaigns. These initiatives play a vital role in helping individuals quit smoking and promoting a healthier, smoke-free lifestyle. However, securing adequate funding for these programs can be a challenge.

One approach to funding smoking cessation programs and public health campaigns is through government support. Governments at the local, state, and federal levels can allocate funds specifically for these initiatives. This can include funding for quit-smoking hotlines, counseling services, and public awareness campaigns. By investing in these programs, governments can significantly reduce smoking rates and improve overall public health.

Another avenue for funding is through private and non-profit organizations. Many companies and foundations are committed to promoting health and wellness, and they may be willing to provide financial support for smoking cessation programs and public health campaigns. Additionally, non-profit organizations dedicated to tobacco control and public health advocacy can also play a crucial role in securing funding for these initiatives.

Furthermore, it is important to explore partnerships and collaborations with healthcare institutions and insurance companies. These entities have a vested interest in reducing smoking rates, as it can lead to significant healthcare cost savings. By partnering with these organizations, smoking cessation programs can secure funding and support for their initiatives.

In addition to traditional funding sources, it is essential to consider innovative approaches to financing smoking cessation programs and public health campaigns. This can include seeking funding from grants, conducting fundraising events, and leveraging social media and crowdfunding platforms to garner financial support from the community.

Ultimately, securing funding for smoking cessation programs and public health campaigns requires a multi-pronged approach. By engaging government support, partnering with private and non-profit organizations, and exploring innovative funding avenues, we can ensure that these critical initiatives have the resources they need to make a meaningful impact on reducing smoking rates and improving public health.

It is important to emphasize the significant return on investment that comes from funding smoking cessation programs and public health campaigns. By reducing smoking rates, we can decrease the burden of tobacco-related diseases, lower healthcare costs, and improve overall productivity and quality of life for individuals. This makes funding for these initiatives not only a public health priority but also a sound economic decision.

In conclusion, funding for smoking cessation programs and public health campaigns is essential for creating a smoke-free future. By securing support from government, private and non-profit organizations, healthcare institutions, and exploring innovative funding approaches, we can ensure that these initiatives have the resources they need to make a meaningful impact. As we continue to prioritize the health and well-being of individuals, investing in these programs is a crucial step towards achieving a smoke-free future for optimal health and wellness.

The impact of taxation on reducing smoking rates

As we delve into the topic of reducing smoking rates, it is imperative to discuss the impact of taxation on this matter. Taxation has been proven to be a powerful tool in curbing smoking rates and promoting a smoke-free future for optimal health and wellness.

One of the most significant effects of taxation on reducing smoking rates is its ability to increase the cost of tobacco products. By imposing higher taxes on cigarettes and other tobacco products, governments can effectively make them less affordable and less accessible to consumers. This, in turn, leads to a decrease in the demand for these products, ultimately resulting in lower smoking rates. Studies have shown that for every 10% increase in the price of cigarettes, there is a corresponding 4% decrease in overall cigarette consumption. This demonstrates the direct correlation between taxation and reduced smoking rates.

Furthermore, taxation also serves as a deterrent for potential smokers, especially among the younger population. Higher prices for tobacco products make them less attractive to individuals who may be considering taking up smoking. This is particularly important as research has shown that the majority of smokers start during their adolescent years. By making tobacco products less affordable, taxation can effectively discourage young people from initiating smoking, thus preventing them from developing a lifelong habit that poses serious health risks.

In addition to reducing smoking rates, taxation also generates significant revenue for governments, which can be allocated towards funding anti-smoking campaigns, cessation programs, and other initiatives aimed at promoting public health and wellness. This creates a positive feedback loop, as the revenue generated from tobacco taxes can be reinvested into efforts to further reduce smoking rates, creating a self-sustaining cycle of progress.

It is important to note that the impact of taxation on reducing smoking rates is not limited to individual countries. In fact, international evidence has shown that higher taxes on tobacco products can lead to significant reductions in smoking prevalence across different regions. This suggests that taxation can be a universally effective strategy in combating smoking and its associated health risks.

Despite the clear benefits of taxation in reducing smoking rates, it is essential for governments to strike a balance in implementing tax policies. Excessive tax increases may lead to undesirable consequences such as black market sales, smuggling, and other illicit activities. Therefore, it is crucial for tax policies to be carefully designed and monitored to ensure their effectiveness in reducing smoking rates without creating unintended negative outcomes.

In conclusion, the impact of taxation on reducing smoking rates is undeniable. By increasing the cost of tobacco products, taxation serves as a powerful deterrent for both current and potential smokers, ultimately leading to lower smoking rates and improved public health. Furthermore, the revenue generated from tobacco taxes can be reinvested into initiatives aimed at further reducing smoking rates, creating a positive feedback loop that promotes a smoke-free future for optimal health and wellness. As we continue to strive towards a smoke-free future, taxation remains a critical tool in our arsenal to combat smoking and its detrimental effects on society.

International efforts to combat smoking and promote a smoke

As we look to the future, it is clear that the global effort to combat smoking and promote a smoke-free world is more important than ever. International organizations, governments, and non-governmental organizations (NGOs) are working together to address the public health crisis caused by tobacco use. Their efforts are focused on a range of strategies, including tobacco control policies, public awareness campaigns, and support for smoking cessation programs.

One of the key international efforts to combat smoking is the World Health Organization's Framework Convention on Tobacco Control (FCTC). This landmark treaty, which was adopted in 2003, has been ratified by 181 countries, making it one of the most widely embraced international health treaties in history. The FCTC sets out a comprehensive set of measures to reduce the demand for tobacco products, including tax and price measures, bans on tobacco advertising and sponsorship, and support for tobacco cessation and treatment programs.

In addition to the FCTC, the World Health Organization (WHO) has launched a number of global initiatives to promote a smoke-free future. These initiatives include the "MPOWER" package of six evidence-based tobacco control measures, which stands for Monitor tobacco use and prevention policies, Protect people from tobacco smoke, Offer help to quit tobacco use, Warn about the dangers of tobacco, Enforce bans on tobacco advertising, promotion and sponsorship, and Raise taxes on tobacco.

At the national level, many countries have implemented their own tobacco control policies and programs. For example, Australia's plain packaging laws require all tobacco products to be sold in plain, standardized packaging with graphic health warnings. This measure has been shown to reduce the appeal of tobacco products and discourage smoking initiation. Other countries have implemented smoke-free laws that prohibit smoking in public places, including bars, restaurants, and workplaces.

Non-governmental organizations (NGOs) also play a critical role in the global effort to combat smoking. Organizations such as the Campaign for Tobacco-Free Kids and the American Cancer Society work to raise awareness about the dangers of tobacco use, advocate for strong tobacco control policies, and support smoking cessation programs. These organizations often work in partnership with governments and international organizations to advance their goals.

In conclusion, the international effort to combat smoking and promote a smoke-free future is a critical public health priority. Through the implementation of comprehensive tobacco control policies, public awareness campaigns, and support for smoking cessation programs, we can work towards a world where everyone can breathe clean, smoke-free air. It is clear that by working together at the international, national, and local levels, we can create a healthier, smoke-free future for all.

Chapter 5: Smoking Cessation Strategies

Nicotine replacement therapy and other cessation aids

As we continue to explore the journey towards a smoke-free future, it is essential to recognize the importance of nicotine replacement therapy (NRT) and other cessation aids in helping individuals break free from the grip of tobacco addiction. NRT has been widely embraced as a valuable tool in the battle against nicotine dependence, offering a range of products designed to alleviate withdrawal symptoms and cravings. These products include nicotine gum, patches, lozenges, inhalers, and nasal sprays, all of which deliver controlled doses of nicotine to the body without the harmful effects of tobacco smoke.

Nicotine replacement therapy works by providing the body with a steady, controlled amount of nicotine, reducing the intensity of withdrawal symptoms and making it easier for individuals to gradually reduce their dependence on the substance. The effectiveness of NRT in aiding smoking cessation has been well-documented, with numerous studies and clinical trials demonstrating its ability to significantly increase the likelihood of long-term abstinence from smoking.

In addition to NRT, there are a variety of other cessation aids available to support individuals on their journey towards a smoke-free life. Prescription medications, such as bupropion and varenicline, have shown promise in helping people quit smoking by targeting the neurochemical pathways involved in nicotine addiction. These medications can help reduce cravings and withdrawal symptoms, making it easier for individuals to resist the urge to smoke.

Behavioral support and counseling are also essential components of a comprehensive smoking cessation program. These interventions can provide individuals with the tools and strategies they need to cope with triggers, manage stress, and develop healthy coping mechanisms. By addressing the psychological and behavioral aspects of tobacco addiction, individuals can increase their chances of successfully quitting smoking for good.

It is important to note that while cessation aids can be valuable tools in the journey towards a smoke-free future, they are most effective when used as part of a comprehensive cessation program that addresses both the physical and psychological aspects of tobacco addiction. By combining NRT or other cessation aids with behavioral support and counseling, individuals can maximize their chances of success and achieve optimal health and wellness.

In conclusion, nicotine replacement therapy and other cessation aids play a crucial role in supporting individuals on their path towards a smoke-free future. These tools can help alleviate withdrawal symptoms, reduce cravings, and increase the likelihood of long-term abstinence from smoking. When used in conjunction with behavioral support and counseling, cessation aids can empower individuals to break free from the grip of tobacco addiction and embrace a healthier, smoke-free life. Embracing a smoke-free future is not only possible but achievable with the right support and resources.

Counseling and support groups for individuals trying to quit

Quitting smoking is a challenging journey, but it is one that is made easier with the support of counseling and support groups. These resources provide valuable guidance and encouragement to individuals looking to embrace a smoke-free future. Counseling offers personalized one-on-one support to address the physical and psychological aspects of nicotine addiction. Trained counselors can help individuals identify their smoking triggers, develop coping strategies, and create a personalized quit plan. They can also provide education on the health risks of smoking and the benefits of quitting, as well as offer techniques to manage nicotine withdrawal symptoms.

Support groups, on the other hand, offer a sense of community and understanding that can be incredibly beneficial for those trying to quit smoking. These groups provide a safe space for individuals to share their experiences, challenges, and successes with others who are on the same journey. Being a part of a support group can help individuals feel less alone in their efforts to quit smoking and can provide them with motivation and accountability. Additionally, support groups often provide access to resources and information about other cessation tools and techniques that can aid in the quitting process.

Both counseling and support groups can be accessed in various ways, including in-person, over the phone, or online. This accessibility allows individuals to choose the format that best suits their needs and preferences. For those who may have limited access to in-person resources, online counseling and support groups can be a valuable alternative. These virtual options provide the same level of support and guidance as in-person resources, allowing individuals to connect with others and receive the help they need from the comfort of their own home.

It is important to note that counseling and support groups are not a one-size-fits-all solution. Different approaches may work better for different individuals, and it may take some trial and error to find the right fit. However, the benefits of seeking out these resources can be significant. Research has shown that individuals who participate in counseling and support groups are more likely to successfully quit smoking compared to those who do not seek out these resources.

In conclusion, counseling and support groups are valuable tools for individuals looking to quit smoking. These resources provide personalized support, a sense of community, and access to valuable information and resources that can aid in the quitting process. Whether accessed in-person, over the phone, or online, counseling and support groups can provide the guidance and encouragement needed to embrace a smoke-free future for optimal health and wellness. If you or someone you know is considering quitting smoking, consider reaching out to a counselor or joining a support group to receive the support needed to succeed in this important journey towards a healthier and smoke-free life.

The importance of setting goals and creating a support network

In the journey towards embracing a smoke-free future, setting clear and achievable goals is paramount. Without a roadmap to guide us, it becomes easy to lose focus and motivation, making it more challenging to stay on track. Setting specific, measurable, attainable, relevant, and time-bound goals provides a sense of direction and purpose, ultimately increasing the likelihood of success. When we have a clear understanding of what we want to achieve and a structured plan to get there, we are better equipped to overcome obstacles and stay committed to our smoke-free journey.

In addition to setting goals, creating a reliable support network can significantly impact our ability to maintain a smoke-free lifestyle. Surrounding ourselves with individuals who understand and respect our goals can provide invaluable encouragement and accountability. Whether it's family members, friends, or support groups, having a network of people who are invested in our success can make a world of difference. They can offer guidance, celebrate our milestones, and provide the necessary motivation during challenging times.

Moreover, having a support network allows us to share our experiences and learn from others who have successfully navigated similar challenges. This sense of community can help us feel less isolated and more empowered as we work towards a smoke-free future. It's important to remember that we don't have to go through this journey alone, and seeking support from others can be instrumental in our success.

Furthermore, a support network can also provide practical assistance in the form of resources, information, and coping strategies. When we encounter triggers or cravings, having someone to turn to for guidance or distraction can prevent us from succumbing to the temptation of smoking. Additionally, being able to lean on others for advice on how to effectively manage stress, anxiety, or other triggers can equip us with the necessary tools to navigate challenging situations without relying on smoking as a coping mechanism.

Ultimately, the combination of setting goals and creating a strong support network can significantly enhance our ability to achieve and maintain a smoke-free lifestyle. By establishing clear objectives and leveraging the encouragement and guidance of others, we can increase our chances of success and experience the optimal health and wellness benefits associated with a smoke-free future.

In conclusion, the importance of setting goals and creating a support network cannot be overstated in the pursuit of a smoke-free future. These two elements work hand in hand to provide us with the structure, motivation, and resources necessary to overcome the challenges associated with quitting smoking. By defining our objectives and enlisting the support of others, we can increase our resilience and determination, ultimately leading us towards a healthier, smoke-free life. As we continue on this journey, let us remember the power of setting goals and the value of a strong support network in realizing our vision of optimal health and wellness.

Overcoming withdrawal symptoms and cravings

As we embrace a smoke-free future for optimal health and wellness, it's crucial to address the challenge of overcoming withdrawal symptoms and cravings. When individuals make the decision to quit smoking, they often experience a range of physical and psychological symptoms as their bodies adjust to the absence of nicotine. These symptoms can include irritability, anxiety, restlessness, and difficulty concentrating. It's important for individuals to understand that these symptoms are temporary and are a natural part of the quitting process.

One effective strategy for managing withdrawal symptoms is to seek support from healthcare professionals, counselors, or support groups. These resources can provide guidance and encouragement as individuals navigate the challenges of quitting smoking. Additionally, there are medications and nicotine replacement therapies available that can help alleviate withdrawal symptoms and cravings. These options should be explored in consultation with a healthcare provider to determine the most appropriate approach for each individual.

In addition to seeking professional support, it's important for individuals to develop healthy coping mechanisms to manage cravings and withdrawal symptoms. Engaging in regular physical activity can help reduce stress and improve mood, making it easier to resist the urge to smoke. Finding alternative activities to replace the habit of smoking, such as chewing gum or practicing deep breathing exercises, can also be helpful in managing cravings.

Furthermore, creating a supportive environment can significantly impact the success of quitting smoking. Surrounding oneself with friends and family who are supportive of the decision to quit can provide the encouragement and motivation needed to stay on track. Removing triggers and temptations from the environment, such as ashtrays and lighters, can also help reduce the likelihood of experiencing cravings.

It's important for individuals to remain patient and persistent as they work through withdrawal symptoms and cravings. The road to a smoke-free future may have its challenges, but the long-term benefits to health and wellness are well worth the effort. By seeking support, exploring medication options, developing healthy coping mechanisms, and creating a supportive environment, individuals can overcome withdrawal symptoms and cravings and embrace a healthier, smoke-free lifestyle.

Chapter 6: The Influence of Advertising and Marketing

The tactics used by tobacco companies to target consumers

Tobacco companies have employed various strategies to target consumers and promote their products, despite the well-documented health risks associated with smoking. These tactics have been carefully designed to appeal to different demographics and create a sense of allure around their products. One of the most insidious tactics used by tobacco companies is the deliberate targeting of vulnerable populations, such as young people and those in lower socioeconomic brackets. By using clever marketing techniques and appealing packaging, these companies aim to entice these groups into starting or continuing smoking habits.

Another tactic employed by tobacco companies is the use of celebrity endorsements and sponsorships to create a sense of glamour and desirability around their products. By associating their brands with popular figures, these companies seek to influence consumers' perceptions and encourage them to view smoking as a fashionable and sophisticated habit. Additionally, tobacco companies have historically invested heavily in advertising and promotional campaigns, utilizing various media platforms to reach a wide audience and perpetuate the image of smoking as a desirable and socially acceptable behavior.

Furthermore, tobacco companies have also engaged in aggressive lobbying efforts to influence public policy and prevent the implementation of regulations that would restrict their ability to market and sell their products. These efforts have included funding research studies to cast doubt on the health risks of smoking, as well as opposing measures aimed at reducing tobacco consumption, such as increased taxation and advertising restrictions. By leveraging their financial resources and political influence, tobacco companies have sought to maintain their foothold in the market and continue profiting from the sale of their products.

In recent years, tobacco companies have also capitalized on the rise of e-cigarettes and other alternative tobacco products as a means of expanding their consumer base. By marketing these products as safer alternatives to traditional cigarettes, these companies have sought to attract new consumers, including young people who may be less inclined to start smoking conventional cigarettes. However, concerns have been raised about the potential health risks associated with these alternative products, as well as their potential to serve as a gateway to traditional smoking.

Overall, the tactics used by tobacco companies to target consumers have been multifaceted and calculated, aimed at perpetuating the allure of smoking and maintaining their market share. Despite increasing awareness of the health risks associated with smoking, these companies continue to employ sophisticated marketing strategies and lobbying efforts to promote their products and influence public perception. As we strive towards a smoke-free future for optimal health and wellness, it is essential to remain vigilant against these tactics and continue working towards reducing tobacco consumption and safeguarding public health.

The impact of tobacco advertising on youth and young adults

Tobacco advertising has a significant influence on youth and young adults, shaping their attitudes and behaviors towards smoking. The pervasive nature of tobacco advertising inundates young people with messages glamorizing smoking, creating a false impression of its desirability and normalcy. This exposure has been shown to increase the likelihood of young people initiating smoking and developing a lifelong tobacco addiction.

The impact of tobacco advertising on youth and young adults is particularly concerning due to the vulnerability of this demographic. Adolescents and young adults are at a critical stage of development, susceptible to external influences and eager to assert their independence.

Tobacco companies capitalize on this vulnerability by strategically targeting young people through advertising campaigns that appeal to their desire for autonomy, rebellion, and social acceptance.

Furthermore, tobacco advertising often portrays smoking as a symbol of maturity, sophistication, and attractiveness, perpetuating harmful stereotypes that entice young individuals seeking to emulate these qualities. This deliberate manipulation of young people's aspirations and self-image through advertising tactics contributes to the normalization of smoking within this demographic, perpetuating the cycle of tobacco addiction.

The proliferation of tobacco advertising across various media platforms further exacerbates its impact on youth and young adults. In the digital age, young people are constantly exposed to tobacco marketing through social media, online content, and influencer endorsements. These platforms enable tobacco companies to infiltrate the daily lives of young individuals, fostering an environment where smoking is portrayed as a commonplace and desirable behavior.

Moreover, tobacco advertising often utilizes appealing imagery, catchy slogans, and celebrity endorsements to captivate the attention of young audiences. These tactics create a powerful association between smoking and positive attributes, leading young people to perceive smoking as a means of achieving the lifestyle and aspirations depicted in these advertisements.

The insidious nature of tobacco advertising's influence on youth and young adults is compounded by the lack of effective regulations to mitigate its impact. While measures such as advertising bans and warning labels have been implemented, tobacco companies continuously adapt their marketing strategies to circumvent these restrictions, perpetuating their influence on young people.

In conclusion, the impact of tobacco advertising on youth and young adults is pervasive and detrimental, perpetuating harmful perceptions of smoking and contributing to the initiation of tobacco use among this demographic. It is imperative to address this issue through comprehensive regulations, education, and advocacy efforts to protect the health and well-being of young individuals and promote a smoke-free future.

Efforts to restrict or ban tobacco advertising

Efforts to restrict or ban tobacco advertising have been a crucial step in the global movement towards a smoke-free future. Advertising plays a significant role in shaping public perception and behavior, and the promotion of tobacco products has long been a contributing factor to the prevalence of smoking. By limiting or prohibiting the advertising of tobacco products, governments and public health organizations aim to reduce the appeal of smoking and discourage individuals from starting or continuing the habit.

Many countries have implemented strict regulations on tobacco advertising, including bans on television, radio, and print advertisements. These restrictions aim to limit the exposure of tobacco products to the general public, particularly to young people who may be more susceptible to the influence of marketing efforts. In addition to traditional media, there has been a growing emphasis on regulating the advertising of tobacco products in digital and social media platforms. The rise of online advertising has presented new challenges in enforcing restrictions, but efforts have been made to address this issue through comprehensive regulations and monitoring mechanisms.

The impact of restricting or banning tobacco advertising has been significant in reducing the prevalence of smoking and promoting public health. Studies have shown that exposure to tobacco advertisements can increase the likelihood of smoking initiation among young people and influence current smokers to continue their habit. By limiting the visibility and promotion of tobacco products, countries have seen a decrease in smoking rates and a shift in societal attitudes towards smoking. Furthermore, restrictions on advertising have contributed to the denormalization of smoking, positioning it as an undesirable behavior rather than a socially acceptable one.

While the efforts to restrict or ban tobacco advertising have been effective in many areas, challenges remain in enforcing these regulations and addressing new forms of marketing. The tobacco industry has continuously sought alternative avenues to promote their products and target specific demographics, including through sponsorships, product placement, and event marketing. This has necessitated ongoing vigilance and adaptation in the regulatory framework to counter these tactics and safeguard public health.

In addition to government action, public health organizations and advocacy groups have played a crucial role in advocating for the restriction or prohibition of tobacco advertising. Through education, awareness campaigns, and policy initiatives, these stakeholders have contributed to raising public consciousness about the harmful effects of smoking and the deceptive nature of tobacco advertising. By mobilizing public support and engaging in dialogue with policymakers, these groups have helped pave the way for stronger regulations and greater accountability within the tobacco industry.

Looking ahead, efforts to restrict or ban tobacco advertising will continue to be an integral component of the broader strategy towards a smoke-free future. As new challenges and opportunities emerge in the evolving landscape of marketing and communication, it is essential to remain vigilant and proactive in addressing the tactics of the tobacco industry. By upholding stringent regulations and fostering a culture of wellness and prevention, societies can move closer towards realizing the vision of a smoke-free world, where optimal health and wellness are prioritized for all.

The role of education in countering the influence of tobacco marketing

As we strive towards a smoke-free future, education plays a crucial role in countering the pervasive influence of tobacco marketing. The power of knowledge and awareness cannot be understated when it comes to combating the tactics used by the tobacco industry to lure individuals, especially the youth, into a harmful and addictive habit.

One of the key aspects of education in this context is providing accurate and comprehensive information about the health risks associated with tobacco use. By arming people with the facts about the detrimental impact of smoking on overall well-being, we can empower them to make informed decisions and resist the allure of tobacco marketing.

Furthermore, education can also shed light on the deceptive strategies employed by tobacco companies to glamorize their products and target vulnerable populations. By teaching individuals to critically analyze and deconstruct marketing messages, we can help them develop a healthy skepticism towards the tactics used to promote tobacco consumption.

In addition to raising awareness about the dangers of tobacco use, education can also equip individuals with the necessary skills to resist peer pressure and social influences that may encourage smoking. By fostering strong decision-making abilities and enhancing self-esteem, education can serve as a powerful tool in building a smoke-free mindset and lifestyle.

Moreover, education can extend beyond formal settings such as schools and encompass public awareness campaigns, community outreach programs, and targeted interventions. By leveraging various platforms to disseminate information and engage with diverse audiences, we can amplify the impact of educational efforts in countering the influence of tobacco marketing.

Ultimately, education serves as a potent antidote to the insidious influence of tobacco marketing, empowering individuals to make choices that prioritize their health and well-being. By promoting a culture of awareness, critical thinking, and resilience, we can pave the way for a future where tobacco marketing holds no sway, and optimal health and wellness prevail.

Chapter 7: The Stigma of Smoking

Addressing societal attitudes towards smoking

As we look towards a smoke-free future, one of the key components to address is the societal attitudes towards smoking. Over the years, smoking has been ingrained into the fabric of many cultures, becoming a social norm and even a symbol of sophistication or rebellion. However, as we continue to gain a better understanding of the detrimental effects of smoking on health and wellness, it is essential to shift these attitudes and perceptions.

One of the first steps in addressing societal attitudes towards smoking is to educate the public about the true consequences of smoking. This involves not only highlighting the immediate health risks such as lung cancer and heart disease, but also shedding light on the long-term impact on overall well-being. By providing accurate and compelling information, we can begin to challenge the misconceptions and myths surrounding smoking.

Moreover, it is crucial to create a supportive environment for those looking to quit smoking. This includes implementing policies and regulations that restrict smoking in public spaces, as well as offering accessible resources for smoking cessation. By making it easier for individuals to break free from the habit, we can gradually shift societal attitudes towards seeing smoking as a negative behavior rather than a socially acceptable one.

In addition, changing societal attitudes towards smoking requires a collaborative effort from various stakeholders, including government agencies, healthcare professionals, and the media. By working together to promote anti-smoking campaigns and initiatives, we can influence public opinion and encourage a collective commitment to embracing a smoke-free future.

Furthermore, it is important to address the influence of the tobacco industry in shaping societal attitudes towards smoking. By exposing the deceptive marketing tactics and manipulative strategies employed by tobacco companies, we can empower individuals to make informed choices and resist the allure of smoking.

Ultimately, the journey towards a smoke-free future is not just about individual behavior change, but also about transforming the cultural and social norms that have perpetuated smoking. By challenging societal attitudes and perceptions, we can pave the way for a healthier and more supportive environment where smoking is no longer the norm, but rather a thing of the past.

The impact of smoking on personal relationships and social interactions

Smoking not only affects the individual's health, but also has a significant impact on personal relationships and social interactions. The habit of smoking can create tension and conflict within relationships, as non-smoking partners may become frustrated with the smoker's habit. This can lead to arguments and strained communication, which can ultimately damage the relationship. In addition, smoking can also restrict social interactions, as many public places and social events are now smoke-free. Smokers may find themselves isolated from their non-smoking friends and family members, as they are forced to step outside in order to smoke. This can lead to feelings of exclusion and alienation, as well as a sense of disconnection from social activities. Furthermore, the smell of smoke can be off-putting to others, which can further strain personal relationships and hinder social interactions.

On a deeper level, smoking can also impact the emotional and psychological dynamics of relationships. Non-smoking partners may worry about the smoker's health and well-being, which can create anxiety and stress within the relationship. This can lead to a lack of trust and understanding, as the non-smoking partner may struggle to empathize with the smoker's addiction. The smoker, in turn, may feel judged and unsupported, leading to feelings of resentment and isolation. These emotional barriers can create a divide between partners, making it difficult to maintain a healthy and supportive relationship.

In terms of social interactions, smoking can limit opportunities for meaningful connections and engagement with others. Smokers may find themselves excluded from certain social activities and events due to their habit, which can lead to feelings of isolation and loneliness. Additionally, the stigma associated with smoking can also impact the way that others perceive and interact with smokers. Non-smokers may be less inclined to engage in conversation or form friendships with smokers, leading to a sense of social exclusion.

It is important to recognize the impact of smoking on personal relationships and social interactions, as this can provide motivation for individuals to make positive changes. By embracing a smoke-free future, individuals can improve their personal relationships and social interactions, leading to greater emotional well-being and a sense of connectedness. Non-smoking partners may feel relieved and supported, while smokers can experience a renewed sense of inclusion and acceptance within their social circles. Ultimately, by choosing to quit smoking, individuals can pave the way for healthier and more fulfilling relationships, as well as a more vibrant and engaging social life. The decision to embrace a smoke-free future is not just about personal health, but also about nurturing and strengthening the connections that enrich our lives.

Overcoming the stigma of being a former smoker

As a professional copywriter with extensive experience in the field of health and wellness, I have dedicated a significant amount of time and effort to addressing the issue of smoking cessation and the challenges that former smokers face. Overcoming the stigma of being a former smoker is a topic that is often overlooked, yet it is a crucial aspect of the journey towards optimal health and wellness.

One of the first steps in overcoming the stigma of being a former smoker is to acknowledge and understand the reasons behind the stigma.

Society often views smoking as a negative habit, and former smokers may be perceived as having a lack of willpower or self-control. Additionally, there may be misconceptions about the difficulty of quitting smoking and the ability of former smokers to maintain their smoke-free status. It is important to address these misconceptions and educate others about the challenges and successes of quitting smoking.

Another important aspect of overcoming the stigma of being a former smoker is to focus on the positive aspects of quitting smoking. Former smokers should be proud of their decision to prioritize their health and well-being. By highlighting the health benefits of quitting smoking, such as improved lung function, reduced risk of various diseases, and increased overall vitality, former smokers can shift the focus from the stigma of their past habits to the positive impact of their current choices.

In addition to focusing on the health benefits, it is important for former smokers to surround themselves with a supportive community. This can include friends, family members, or support groups who understand and appreciate the challenges of quitting smoking. By building a strong support network, former smokers can feel more confident in their decision and reduce the impact of any lingering stigma from their past smoking habits.

Furthermore, it is essential for former smokers to adopt a positive mindset and approach towards their smoke-free future. This involves reframing their identity from that of a smoker to that of a non-smoker. By embracing their new identity and focusing on the positive changes in their life, former smokers can overcome any internalized stigma and stand proud in their decision to quit smoking.

In conclusion, overcoming the stigma of being a former smoker is a multifaceted process that requires understanding, education, support, and a positive mindset. By addressing the reasons behind the stigma, focusing on the health benefits of quitting smoking, building a supportive community, and embracing a positive identity, former smokers can confidently navigate their smoke-free future and prioritize their optimal health and wellness. It is my hope that by shedding light on this topic, we can empower former smokers to embrace their smoke-free future with pride and confidence.

Promoting empathy and support for individuals trying to quit

As we continue to move towards a smoke-free future, it is essential to promote empathy and support for individuals who are trying to quit smoking. Quitting smoking is a challenging journey that requires determination, strength, and support from loved ones and the community. It's important to understand the struggles and difficulties that individuals face when trying to quit smoking, and to offer them the empathy and support they need to succeed.

One way to promote empathy and support for individuals trying to quit smoking is to create a supportive environment that encourages open communication and understanding. This can be achieved through education and awareness campaigns that highlight the struggles of quitting smoking and the benefits of a smoke-free lifestyle. By raising awareness and promoting empathy, we can help reduce the stigma associated with quitting smoking and create a more supportive and understanding community for those who are trying to quit.

In addition to raising awareness, it's important to provide practical support for individuals who are trying to quit smoking. This can include access to smoking cessation programs, counseling services, and support groups. By providing access to these resources, we can help individuals develop the skills and strategies they need to successfully quit smoking and maintain a smoke-free lifestyle.

Furthermore, it's crucial to offer emotional support and encouragement to individuals who are trying to quit smoking. Quitting smoking can be a highly emotional and challenging experience, and individuals need the support and understanding of their loved ones and the community. By offering empathy, understanding, and encouragement, we can help individuals stay motivated and committed to their goal of quitting smoking.

It's also important to recognize and celebrate the progress and achievements of individuals who are trying to quit smoking. Quitting smoking is a significant accomplishment, and individuals should be acknowledged and praised for their efforts. By celebrating their progress, we can help individuals stay motivated and inspired to continue on their journey towards a smoke-free future.

In conclusion, promoting empathy and support for individuals trying to quit smoking is essential in creating a supportive and understanding environment for those who are on the path to a smoke-free future. By raising awareness, providing practical support, offering emotional encouragement, and celebrating achievements, we can help individuals successfully quit smoking and embrace a healthier and smoke-free lifestyle. It's time to come together as a community and support each other in this journey towards optimal health and wellness.

Chapter 8: The Global Impact of Smoking

The prevalence of smoking in different countries and regions

Smoking is a global issue that affects people from all walks of life. The prevalence of smoking varies widely from country to country and even within different regions of the same country. According to the World Health Organization, the highest rates of smoking are found in Eastern Europe, where nearly one in every three adults smokes. In contrast, the lowest rates of smoking are found in the Middle East and Africa, where less than 10% of adults smoke.

In the United States, the prevalence of smoking has declined significantly over the past few decades, but it still remains a major public health concern. According to the Centers for Disease Control and Prevention, approximately 14% of adults in the United States are smokers. However, there are significant disparities in smoking rates among different demographic groups. For example, smoking rates are higher among individuals with lower levels of education and income, as well as among certain racial and ethnic groups.

In Europe, smoking rates also vary widely from country to country. For example, in Greece, nearly 40% of adults smoke, while in Sweden, the rate is less than 10%. These variations can be attributed to a variety of factors, including cultural attitudes towards smoking, government policies on tobacco control, and socioeconomic conditions.

In Asia, smoking rates are also diverse. In countries like Indonesia and the Philippines, smoking rates are high, with approximately 40% of adults being smokers. In contrast, in countries like Singapore and South Korea, smoking rates are much lower, at around 15%. These variations can be attributed to factors such as the availability and affordability of tobacco products, as well as cultural norms and attitudes towards smoking.

In Africa, smoking rates are generally lower compared to other regions, with the exception of countries like South Africa and Namibia, where smoking rates are higher, at around 20%. The low prevalence of smoking in many African countries can be attributed to a variety of factors, including limited access to tobacco products, strong social and cultural norms against smoking, and government policies on tobacco control.

Overall, the prevalence of smoking varies widely from country to country and region to region, and is influenced by a complex interplay of cultural, social, economic, and political factors. It is important for public health authorities and policymakers to understand these variations in order to develop targeted interventions and policies to reduce smoking rates and promote a smoke-free future for optimal health and wellness.

The disparities in smoking rates among different demographics

Smoking rates vary significantly among different demographics, with certain groups experiencing higher rates of tobacco use than others. These disparities are influenced by a variety of factors, including socioeconomic status, education level, and cultural background. Understanding the reasons behind these disparities is crucial for developing targeted interventions and policies to reduce smoking rates across all demographics.

One of the most significant disparities in smoking rates is observed across socioeconomic lines. Individuals with lower income levels are more likely to smoke than those with higher incomes. This disparity is often attributed to the higher levels of stress and limited access to resources for smoking cessation in lower-income communities. Additionally, individuals with lower levels of education are more likely to smoke, reflecting the impact of education on health behaviors.

Cultural background also plays a role in smoking disparities, with certain racial and ethnic groups experiencing higher rates of tobacco use. For example, American Indian and Alaska Native communities have some of the highest smoking rates in the United States, while Asian Americans have lower smoking rates compared to the general population. These disparities are influenced by cultural norms, historical factors, and targeted marketing by tobacco companies.

Gender is another important demographic factor that influences smoking rates. Historically, smoking rates have been higher among men than women. However, the gap has narrowed in recent years, and in some younger age groups, female smoking rates are now higher than male rates. Understanding these shifting patterns is essential for designing effective tobacco control strategies that address the needs of both men and women.

Age is also a key demographic factor in smoking disparities. While smoking rates have declined overall in recent decades, certain age groups, such as young adults, continue to have higher rates of tobacco use. This is partly due to targeted marketing by the tobacco industry and social influences among peer groups. Additionally, older adults who have been smoking for many years may face unique challenges in quitting, highlighting the need for targeted cessation programs for this demographic.

Addressing disparities in smoking rates requires a multifaceted approach that takes into account the unique needs and challenges of different demographics. This includes implementing policies that reduce the availability and appeal of tobacco products, providing accessible and culturally sensitive cessation resources, and addressing the social determinants of health that contribute to smoking disparities.

Furthermore, targeted public health campaigns can raise awareness about the specific risks of smoking within different demographic groups and promote culturally relevant messages about the benefits of quitting. By tailoring interventions to the specific needs of different demographics, we can work towards a smoke-free future that promotes optimal health and wellness for all.

The impact of smoking on global health and healthcare systems

Smoking has a profound impact on global health and healthcare systems. The detrimental effects of smoking on individuals' health are well-documented, but the impact of smoking extends beyond the individual to the broader healthcare system and society as a whole.

First and foremost, smoking is a leading cause of preventable death worldwide. The World Health Organization (WHO) estimates that tobacco use kills more than 8 million people each year. This places a significant burden on healthcare systems, as resources are allocated to treat smoking-related illnesses such as lung cancer, heart disease, and chronic obstructive pulmonary disease (COPD). These conditions require intensive and often long-term medical care, placing strain on healthcare facilities and personnel.

In addition to the direct health consequences, smoking also has economic implications for healthcare systems. The costs associated with treating smoking-related illnesses are substantial, including hospitalization, medication, and rehabilitation. Furthermore, the loss of productivity due to smoking-related illnesses further impacts the economy and healthcare systems.

The impact of smoking on global health is not limited to physical health. Mental health is also affected, as smoking has been linked to increased rates of depression and anxiety. This has implications for mental healthcare systems, as resources are diverted to address the mental health consequences of smoking.

Furthermore, the impact of smoking is not evenly distributed across the global population. Low- and middle-income countries bear a disproportionate burden of smoking-related illness and healthcare costs. This exacerbates existing healthcare disparities and further strains already limited healthcare resources.

Addressing the impact of smoking on global health and healthcare systems requires a comprehensive and multi-faceted approach. This includes implementing evidence-based tobacco control policies, such as tobacco taxation, smoke-free legislation, and comprehensive tobacco cessation programs. These measures have been shown to reduce smoking rates and mitigate the burden on healthcare systems.

In addition to policy interventions, public health campaigns and education are essential in raising awareness about the impact of smoking and promoting smoking cessation. By empowering individuals with knowledge and resources, the prevalence of smoking can be reduced, thereby alleviating the strain on healthcare systems.

Furthermore, investment in research and development of smoking cessation interventions is crucial in addressing the impact of smoking on global health. This includes the development of innovative cessation therapies and technologies, as well as the integration of smoking cessation into routine healthcare practices.

In conclusion, the impact of smoking on global health and healthcare systems is profound and multi-faceted. It places a significant burden on healthcare resources, exacerbates existing healthcare disparities, and has implications for both physical and mental health. Addressing this impact requires a comprehensive approach that includes policy interventions, public health campaigns, education, and research. By embracing a smoke-free future, we can optimize health and wellness on a global scale.

International efforts to reduce smoking and promote a smoke

As we look towards a smoke-free future, it is crucial to examine the international efforts that have been made to reduce smoking and promote a healthier lifestyle. Across the globe, there has been a concerted push to educate the public about the dangers of smoking and to implement policies that discourage its use.

One of the most significant international efforts has been the implementation of tobacco control measures by the World Health Organization (WHO). The WHO has worked with countries around the world to develop and implement strategies aimed at reducing the prevalence of smoking. These efforts have included initiatives to increase public awareness of the health risks associated with smoking, as well as measures to regulate the marketing and sale of tobacco products.

In addition to the efforts of the WHO, many countries have also taken steps to implement their own tobacco control policies. These policies may include restrictions on where smoking is allowed, increased taxes on tobacco products, and public education campaigns. By taking a comprehensive approach to tobacco control, these countries have been able to make significant strides in reducing smoking rates and promoting a smoke-free environment.

Another important international effort to reduce smoking has been the implementation of smoke-free laws and regulations. These laws are designed to protect non-smokers from the harmful effects of secondhand smoke and to create environments that are conducive to quitting smoking. By implementing smoke-free laws, countries have been able to create healthier public spaces and workplaces, and to reduce the overall prevalence of smoking.

Furthermore, international organizations and advocacy groups have played a crucial role in promoting a smoke-free future. These organizations work to raise awareness of the health risks associated with smoking, to advocate for policies that reduce smoking rates, and to provide support for those looking to quit smoking. By working together, these groups have been able to amplify their impact and create a united front against smoking.

In conclusion, the international efforts to reduce smoking and promote a smoke-free future have been crucial in addressing the global public health crisis caused by smoking. By working together, countries, organizations, and advocates have been able to make significant strides in reducing smoking rates and creating environments that support optimal health and wellness. As we continue to move towards a smoke-free future, it is imperative that we build on these efforts and continue to prioritize the health and well-being of all individuals.

Chapter 9: The Role of Healthcare Professionals

The importance of healthcare providers in promoting smoking cessation

Healthcare providers play a crucial role in promoting smoking cessation and helping individuals embrace a smoke-free future for optimal health and wellness. As trusted sources of information and guidance, healthcare professionals have the knowledge and expertise to educate and support patients in their journey towards quitting smoking.

One of the key responsibilities of healthcare providers is to assess and evaluate the smoking habits of their patients. By taking the time to understand the frequency and intensity of smoking, as well as any previous attempts to quit, healthcare professionals can tailor their approach to best support the individual's needs. This personalized approach is essential in addressing the unique challenges and barriers that each patient may face when trying to quit smoking.

In addition to assessment, healthcare providers also play a vital role in providing evidence-based interventions to help patients quit smoking. This may include counseling, behavioral therapies, and medication management. By offering a comprehensive approach to smoking cessation, healthcare professionals can increase the likelihood of successful long-term quitting.

Furthermore, healthcare providers can also serve as advocates for smoke-free policies and initiatives within their communities. By raising awareness about the dangers of smoking and the benefits of quitting, healthcare professionals can help create a supportive environment for individuals looking to make positive changes in their lives. This can include partnering with local organizations and public health campaigns to promote smoking cessation and encourage healthier lifestyles.

Another important aspect of the role of healthcare providers in promoting smoking cessation is the provision of ongoing support and follow-up care. Quitting smoking is a challenging process, and patients may experience setbacks along the way. Healthcare professionals can offer encouragement, resources, and ongoing monitoring to help patients stay on track and maintain their commitment to quitting.

In conclusion, healthcare providers play a critical role in promoting smoking cessation and supporting individuals in their journey towards a smoke-free future. By assessing smoking habits, providing evidence-based interventions, advocating for smoke-free policies, and offering ongoing support, healthcare professionals can make a significant impact on the health and wellness of their patients. Their knowledge, expertise, and dedication are essential in helping individuals embrace a healthier, smoke-free lifestyle.

Implementing screening and intervention protocols for smoking

As we continue to move towards a smoke-free future, it is crucial to implement effective screening and intervention protocols for smoking. These protocols are essential in identifying individuals who are at risk for smoking-related health issues and providing them with the necessary support and resources to quit smoking.

Screening for smoking is an important step in identifying individuals who may be at risk for developing smoking-related health issues. This can be done through various methods, including questionnaires, interviews, and physical exams. By identifying individuals who are at risk for smoking, healthcare professionals can intervene early and provide them with the necessary support to quit smoking.

Once individuals have been identified as being at risk for smoking, it is important to intervene and provide them with the necessary support and resources to quit. This can include counseling, medication, and support groups. By providing individuals with the necessary support and resources, healthcare professionals can increase the likelihood of successful smoking cessation.

It is also important to provide ongoing support and follow-up to individuals who are trying to quit smoking. This can help to ensure that they stay on track and continue to abstain from smoking. By providing ongoing support and follow-up, healthcare professionals can increase the likelihood of long-term smoking cessation.

In addition to providing support for individuals who are trying to quit smoking, it is also important to implement policies and programs that promote a smoke-free environment. This can include implementing smoke-free policies in public places, workplaces, and other settings. By creating a smoke-free environment, we can reduce the prevalence of smoking and protect non-smokers from the harmful effects of secondhand smoke.

In conclusion, implementing screening and intervention protocols for smoking is essential in our journey towards a smoke-free future. By identifying individuals who are at risk for smoking and providing them with the necessary support and resources to quit, we can improve the health and wellness of our communities. Additionally, by creating smoke-free environments, we can further reduce the prevalence of smoking and protect non-smokers from the harmful effects of secondhand smoke. It is crucial that we continue to prioritize these efforts in order to achieve optimal health and wellness for all.

The impact of smoking on healthcare costs and resources

Smoking has a significant and undeniable impact on healthcare costs and resources. The adverse effects of smoking on overall health lead to a substantial burden on healthcare systems worldwide. The financial implications of smoking-related illnesses are staggering, with billions of dollars spent annually on medical care, treatment, and hospitalization for smokers and non-smokers exposed to secondhand smoke.

The direct healthcare costs associated with smoking are substantial. Individuals who smoke tend to require more frequent medical attention and treatment for a wide range of health issues, including respiratory diseases, cardiovascular conditions, and various types of cancer. The expenses related to physician visits, prescription medications, and hospital stays for smoking-related illnesses place a heavy strain on healthcare budgets. Additionally, the long-term care and management of chronic conditions caused by smoking contribute to the escalating costs of healthcare.

Furthermore, smoking also has a significant impact on resources within the healthcare system. The demand for medical services and facilities increases as a result of smoking-related illnesses, leading to overcrowded emergency rooms, longer wait times for appointments, and a strain on healthcare providers. In addition, the allocation of resources such as medical equipment, supplies, and personnel is heavily influenced by the prevalence of smoking-related conditions, diverting attention and resources away from other areas of healthcare.

The economic burden of smoking extends beyond direct healthcare costs and resource allocation. The indirect costs of smoking, including lost productivity, absenteeism from work, and disability, further strain the healthcare system and the economy as a whole. The impact of smoking on healthcare costs and resources is a complex issue that requires a comprehensive approach to address effectively.

Efforts to reduce the prevalence of smoking and promote a smoke-free future are essential for mitigating the impact on healthcare costs and resources. Implementing comprehensive tobacco control measures, such as public health campaigns, smoking cessation programs, and tobacco taxation, can help reduce the burden of smoking-related illnesses on healthcare systems. By preventing smoking initiation and supporting smokers in quitting, the healthcare costs and resource utilization associated with smoking can be significantly reduced.

In conclusion, the impact of smoking on healthcare costs and resources is profound and multifaceted. The financial implications of smoking-related illnesses place a heavy burden on healthcare budgets, while the demand for medical services and resources continues to grow. Addressing the impact of smoking on healthcare costs and resources requires a concerted effort to reduce smoking prevalence and support cessation efforts. Embracing a smoke-free future is essential for optimal health and wellness, as well as for the sustainability of healthcare systems worldwide.

Training and education for healthcare professionals on smoking cessation

As we look towards a smoke-free future for optimal health and wellness, it is crucial to emphasize the importance of training and education for healthcare professionals on smoking cessation. Healthcare professionals play a pivotal role in helping individuals quit smoking and embrace a healthier lifestyle. By equipping them with the necessary knowledge and skills, we can enhance their ability to effectively support patients in their journey towards quitting smoking.

Training and education for healthcare professionals on smoking cessation should encompass a comprehensive understanding of the physiological and psychological aspects of nicotine addiction. This includes the impact of smoking on overall health, the addictive nature of nicotine, and the various cessation methods and treatment options available. In addition, healthcare professionals should be trained to effectively communicate with patients about smoking cessation, addressing any concerns or barriers that may arise.

Furthermore, it is essential for healthcare professionals to stay updated on the latest research and evidence-based practices in smoking cessation. This involves attending continuing education programs, workshops, and conferences focused on tobacco control and cessation strategies. By staying informed about the most effective approaches to smoking cessation, healthcare professionals can better assist their patients in achieving long-term success in quitting smoking.

In addition to theoretical knowledge, practical skills are equally important in training healthcare professionals on smoking cessation. This includes learning how to conduct brief interventions, provide counseling, and prescribe appropriate cessation medications. Moreover, healthcare professionals should be proficient in developing personalized cessation plans tailored to each patient's unique needs and circumstances.

An essential aspect of training and education for healthcare professionals on smoking cessation is the promotion of a patient-centered approach. This involves recognizing the individuality of each patient and tailoring cessation interventions accordingly. Healthcare professionals should be trained to provide non-judgmental support, motivate patients, and empower them to take control of their smoking habits.

Moreover, interprofessional collaboration is crucial in the context of smoking cessation. Training for healthcare professionals should emphasize the importance of working collaboratively with other professionals such as psychologists, social workers, and pharmacists to provide comprehensive care for individuals seeking to quit smoking. By fostering a multidisciplinary approach, healthcare professionals can address the diverse needs of patients and enhance the effectiveness of smoking cessation interventions.

Another vital aspect of training and education for healthcare professionals on smoking cessation is the integration of technology and innovative tools. This includes training on how to utilize mobile applications, telemedicine, and other digital resources to support patients in their cessation journey. By leveraging technology, healthcare professionals can extend their reach, provide ongoing support, and monitor the progress of patients remotely.

In conclusion, training and education for healthcare professionals on smoking cessation is a critical component of promoting a smoke-free future for optimal health and wellness. By equipping healthcare professionals with comprehensive knowledge, practical skills, and a patient-centered approach, we can enhance their ability to effectively support individuals in quitting smoking. Moreover, promoting interprofessional collaboration and leveraging technology are essential strategies to further strengthen the capacity of healthcare professionals in addressing smoking cessation. Ultimately, investing in the training and education of healthcare professionals in smoking cessation will contribute to reducing the prevalence of smoking and improving the overall health outcomes of individuals and communities.

Chapter 10: Embracing a Smoke-Free Future

Celebrating success stories of individuals who have quit smoking

Quitting smoking is a monumental achievement that deserves to be celebrated. For many individuals, the journey to becoming smoke-free is not easy, but their success stories serve as inspiration for others who are still struggling to break free from the grip of tobacco addiction. These success stories are a testament to the power of determination and the resilience of the human spirit. They remind us that it is possible to overcome even the most challenging obstacles and emerge victorious on the other side.

One such success story is that of Sarah, who had been a smoker for over 20 years before she made the decision to quit. She had tried to quit multiple times in the past, but it wasn't until she found the right support system and developed a personalized quitting plan that she was able to finally kick the habit for good. Sarah's journey was filled with ups and downs, but through sheer determination and the support of her loved ones, she was able to overcome the cravings and live a smoke-free life.

Another inspiring success story is that of Michael, who had been a pack-a-day smoker for over a decade. He had always wanted to quit, but the fear of withdrawal symptoms and the uncertainty of life without cigarettes held him back. It wasn't until he experienced a health scare that he realized he needed to make a change. With the help of a smoking cessation program and the support of his healthcare provider, Michael was able to successfully quit smoking and reclaim his health.

These success stories are not isolated incidents. They are a testament to the fact that anyone can quit smoking with the right support and resources. They serve as a beacon of hope for those who are still struggling with their addiction, showing them that it is possible to break free and live a healthier, smoke-free life.

Celebrating these success stories is important because it not only honors the accomplishments of the individuals who have overcome their addiction but also serves as motivation for others who are still on their journey to becoming smoke-free. By sharing these stories, we can inspire and empower others to take the necessary steps to quit smoking and embrace a healthier lifestyle.

In conclusion, the success stories of individuals who have quit smoking are a powerful reminder of the strength of the human spirit and the possibility of overcoming even the most challenging obstacles. These stories serve as inspiration for those who are still struggling with their addiction, showing them that it is possible to break free and live a healthier, smoke-free life. By celebrating these success stories, we can empower and motivate others to take the necessary steps to quit smoking and embrace a brighter, healthier future.

The potential for a future without tobacco

As we look towards the future, it's important to consider the potential for a world without tobacco. The impact of tobacco use on public health and wellness is undeniable, and the prospect of a smoke-free future is one that holds great promise for optimal health and well-being.

One of the key benefits of a future without tobacco is the potential for a significant reduction in the prevalence of smoking-related diseases. Tobacco use is a leading cause of preventable death and disease worldwide, and eliminating it from our society could have a profound impact on public health. By reducing the number of individuals who are exposed to the harmful effects of tobacco, we can potentially lower the incidence of conditions such as lung cancer, heart disease, and respiratory illnesses.

Furthermore, a smoke-free future has the potential to improve air quality and reduce environmental pollution. Tobacco smoke contains a myriad of harmful chemicals and toxins that can have a detrimental impact on the air we breathe and the environment as a whole. By eliminating tobacco use, we can decrease the amount of pollutants in the atmosphere and create a cleaner, healthier environment for future generations.

In addition to the health and environmental benefits, a future without tobacco also holds promise for economic prosperity. The costs associated with treating smoking-related diseases and addressing the environmental impact of tobacco use are substantial. By reducing the prevalence of tobacco use, we can potentially lower healthcare expenditures and redirect resources towards more productive and beneficial endeavors.

Furthermore, the cultivation and production of tobacco are associated with a range of social and economic challenges, including child labor, deforestation, and the exploitation of vulnerable communities. By moving towards a tobacco-free future, we can potentially address these issues and create a more equitable and sustainable global economy.

It's important to acknowledge that achieving a smoke-free future will require concerted efforts and collaborative action on multiple fronts. This includes implementing and enforcing effective tobacco control policies, promoting public awareness and education, and providing support for individuals who are looking to quit smoking.

In conclusion, the potential for a future without tobacco is one that holds great promise for the health, well-being, and prosperity of individuals and societies around the world. By reducing the prevalence of smoking-related diseases, improving air quality, and addressing the economic and social challenges associated with tobacco use, we can create a world that is healthier, cleaner, and more equitable for all. Embracing a smoke-free future is a critical step towards realizing optimal health and wellness for ourselves and future generations.

The importance of continued advocacy and support for a smoke

As we look towards a smoke-free future, it is crucial to recognize the importance of continued advocacy and support for this cause. The journey towards a healthier, smoke-free world is ongoing, and it requires the dedication and commitment of individuals, organizations, and governments at all levels. Advocacy plays a vital role in raising awareness, shaping public opinion, and influencing policy changes that can further promote a smoke-free environment.

One of the key aspects of continued advocacy is the education of the public about the harmful effects of smoking and the benefits of a smoke-free lifestyle. By providing accurate information and dispelling myths and misconceptions, advocates can empower individuals to make informed choices about their health. This education also extends to younger generations, as it is crucial to prevent the initiation of smoking among adolescents and young adults.

Support for a smoke-free future also involves creating and implementing policies that restrict smoking in public spaces, workplaces, and other environments where non-smokers may be exposed to secondhand smoke. These policies not only protect non-smokers from the harmful effects of secondhand smoke but also encourage smokers to consider quitting. Additionally, providing access to smoking cessation resources and support services is essential in helping individuals who are ready to embrace a smoke-free lifestyle.

Furthermore, continued advocacy and support for a smoke-free future require collaboration across various sectors, including healthcare, public health, education, and business. By working together, these sectors can leverage their respective resources and expertise to advance the goals of a smoke-free society. This collaboration also extends to engaging with policymakers to ensure that regulations and legislation align with the objective of reducing tobacco use and promoting public health.

In addition to education and policy changes, advocacy for a smoke-free future involves challenging the influence of the tobacco industry and countering its marketing and promotional efforts. By exposing the tactics used by the tobacco industry to target vulnerable populations and glamorize smoking, advocates can help to reduce the appeal of tobacco products and prevent the uptake of smoking among new generations.

It is important to recognize that advocacy for a smoke-free future is a long-term commitment that requires persistence and resilience. While significant progress has been made in reducing smoking rates and creating smoke-free environments, there is still much work to be done. Continued advocacy and support are essential in maintaining momentum and addressing emerging challenges, such as the use of alternative tobacco products and the impact of tobacco industry tactics in low- and middle-income countries.

Ultimately, the importance of continued advocacy and support for a smoke-free future cannot be overstated. It is a collective effort that requires the involvement of individuals, communities, and institutions to create a healthier and safer environment for all. By remaining steadfast in our commitment to this cause, we can work towards a future where smoking is no longer the leading cause of preventable illness and death, and where optimal health and wellness are attainable for everyone.

The role of individuals, communities, and governments in creating a smoke

As we embrace a smoke-free future for optimal health and wellness, it is essential to understand the role of individuals, communities, and governments in creating a smoke-free environment. Each of these entities plays a critical role in shaping the future of public health and ensuring that everyone has the opportunity to live in a clean and healthy environment.

Individuals have the power to make a significant impact on the smoke-free movement. By making the personal choice to refrain from smoking and supporting smoke-free policies, individuals can create a positive change in their communities. They can also serve as role models for others, especially young people, by demonstrating the benefits of living a smoke-free lifestyle. In addition, individuals can also advocate for smoke-free policies in their workplaces, public spaces, and even in their own homes, further promoting a healthy and clean environment for everyone.

Communities also have a vital role to play in creating a smoke-free future. Through grassroots efforts and community organizing, local residents can work together to advocate for smoke-free policies and educate others about the benefits of living in a smoke-free environment. Community leaders and organizations can also play a significant role in promoting smoke-free initiatives, providing resources and support to individuals and businesses who are committed to creating a healthier community for all.

At the governmental level, policymakers have a responsibility to enact and enforce smoke-free policies that protect the health and well-being of their constituents. This includes implementing laws and regulations that restrict smoking in public places, workplaces, and multi-unit housing, as well as providing support for smoking cessation programs and resources. Governments can also allocate funding for public education campaigns that raise awareness about the dangers of smoking and the benefits of living in a smoke-free environment.

By working together, individuals, communities, and governments can create a smoke-free future that promotes optimal health and wellness for all. It requires a collective effort to change social norms, promote healthy behaviors, and create policies that support a smoke-free environment. It is essential for everyone to recognize their role in this movement and to take action to ensure that future generations can live in a world free from the harmful effects of tobacco smoke.

In conclusion, the role of individuals, communities, and governments in creating a smoke-free future cannot be overstated. Each of these entities has a unique and essential role to play in shaping the future of public health and wellness. By working together and taking decisive action, we can create a world where everyone has the opportunity to live in a clean and healthy environment, free from the dangers of tobacco smoke. It is up to each of us to embrace this vision and work towards a smoke-free future for the well-being of all.

Don't miss out!

Visit the website below and you can sign up to receive emails whenever Juanita LA publishes a new book. There's no charge and no obligation.

https://books2read.com/r/B-A-WEQOC-TMIDF

BOOKS 2 READ

Connecting independent readers to independent writers.

Did you love *Clearing the Air*? Then you should read *Smoke-Free*[1] by Juanita LA!

Welcome to "Smoke-Free: Breaking the Habit and Embracing a Healthier Life." In this book, we will explore the journey of breaking free from the grip of smoking and embracing a healthier, smoke-free life. As an experienced author and advocate for health and wellness, I have dedicated my career to helping individuals overcome their addiction to smoking and live a life free from the harmful effects of tobacco.

Smoking is a widespread and deeply ingrained habit that affects millions of people worldwide. Despite the well-documented risks and dangers associated with smoking, many individuals struggle to break free from its addictive hold. The physical, emotional, and psychological dependency on nicotine can make it incredibly challenging to quit

---

1. https://books2read.com/u/mdavkR

2. https://books2read.com/u/mdavkR

smoking, but it is not impossible. With the right support, guidance, and determination, anyone can break the habit and embrace a smoke-free lifestyle.

Also by Juanita LA

Smoke-Free for Life
Break the Habit
Smoke-Free
Clearing the Air

Milton Keynes UK
Ingram Content Group UK Ltd.
UKHW042238011124
450424UK00001BA/80